The merry-go-round

Story by Beverley Randell
Illustrated by Liz Alger

"Come here, James,"
said Dad.
"Come here, Kate.
Come here, Nick.
Look at the merry-go-round."

Look at James.

James is up on a pig.

Look at Kate.

Kate is up on a duck.

Dad said,
"Here is a car, Nick."

"No!" said Nick.

Dad said,

"Here is a plane, Nick."

"No!" said Nick.

"A horse! Look!
A horse!" said Nick.
"Here is a horse."

13

James is up on a pig.

Kate is up on a duck.

Nick is up on a **horse**.